Deception: When Everything You Know about God is Wrong

Dan Desmarques

Published by 22 Lions Bookstore, 2019.

Copyright Page

Deception: When Everything You Know about God is Wrong

By Dan Desmarques

Copyright © Dan Desmarques, 2019 (1st Ed.). All Rights Reserved.

Published by 22 Lions Bookstore and Publishing House

About the Publisher

About the 22 Lions Bookstore:

www.22Lions.com

Facebook.com/22Lions

Twitter.com/22lionsbookshop

Instagram.com/22lionsbookshop

Pinterest.com/22lionsbookshop

Introduction

What if everything you believed to be true was a lie? What if the only reason why it seems that religion has failed on you, is because you have been hearing lies that do not match the real God? What if the truth has been remaining hidden from you on purpose? And what if you could forgive yourself for being deceived? What if you could change your life by getting access to the real truth? For this is what this book proposes you, while answering all these questions. Here, you will obtain a direct guidance filled with personal examples, on how christians and many other religious groups are corrupted and end up corrupting others along the way, pushing them further away from the truth that God wishes everyone to know. This truth is so important, that without it, you will never know why the life of so many seems so chaotic and without a positive end, despite all the prayers and dedication to rituals of various nature. In fact, if you wish to become more religious, this book can help you correct your practice towards this truth, while avoiding being deceived as so many others have been. For this is the truth that God wishes you to access through your own existence, with your own awareness and ethics, and not just a blind faith.

The Realm of the Living Dead

When people walk outside, immersed in their own thoughts, they forget that they are part of a collective. And then what happens is that, they become selfish, self-centered, and ignore the rights of others. And when this occurs, they obtain problems in return, which they never assume to be caused by themselves. That is the real meaning of karma — self-caused harm.

If people were not so selfish, if the vast majority cooperated more for the common good, their life would be much better. Because if everyone shared their own personal interests, their own information and viewpoints, motivated by a will in improving society and in helping others, then this society would give them back too, as that's individual good multiplied by everyone else.

As you see, most people don't really understand life, as much as they don't understand that the purpose of their job is not to have a salary, but to help someone; because, the only reason their job exists, is that their job is helping others. And that's why they can't understand as well, when unemployed, that nobody has the obligation to give them a job that society doesn't need, or for which there are enough and better helpers already employed and doing the same; they don't understand that the acquisition of a skill is always related to the need in the world for such skill. And along this line, they can't see that the world cooperates for a common good.

When people believe that life is a competition, and about trying to pull others down in order to survive, in order to get more, they don't see that they get less by default. As a matter of fact, competition leads to jealousy, and jealousy leads to lack of appreciation, which then leads to the negative idea of unfairness and hatred towards the world, guiding our heart towards vibrating at a lower frequency, which then brings us to a personal reality of having less than what we already have. This is why Christ has said: "Whoever does not have, even what he has will be taken from him." (Matthew 13:12). The idea of scarcity and hatred towards the rich, always leads to more poverty, because it comes from a standpoint of lower vibration. What you believe and what you feel, you attract; and so, if you believe that you are poor because someone else is rich, and you

DECEPTION

hate that reality which you would like to have, envy and differentiation before it literally shapes your energy towards more of what you don't want.

We could all get much more if we were cooperating with one another, first in our heart, with appreciation, and then in our spirit with belief in a greater good, and in God to guide us there. We don't need to be accepted and respected to do these three things. The hate of another being does not need to change your respect for him, and his arrogance does not need to change your love.

You need to understand that most people, with either abundance or scarcity, live under the veil of ignorance, ignorance in what regards the source of their wealth, the similarities between their nature and the one of others, and the shifts in the energy field, that can make one who was poor, become very rich, and the one who was very rich, become very poor in the next day.

The Causes of Our Deception

How do you deal with the ignorant mindset of the masses? Well, this is what ignorance basically means. You can't argue with the fools. To exemplify this, I once told a former girlfriend that she should listen to me because I wrote more than three hundred books and managed several companies, and her reply was: "Your knowledge is old fashioned and I watch reality shows." And, how can anyone answer that? The level of stupidity and arrogance is such, that is really hard to argue anything against it. And yet, interestingly, I did meet some of the people who go on these TV shows, for they have sought many important answers to life through me. I met them personally and know, for a fact, how ignorant they are. And I also know how hard they improved themselves, not in reading books, but in training themselves in public speaking and the art of bullshitting in public with confidence. Because that's what pretending to know what you don't truly means, especially when you think you can go on television and express your opinion to the dumb masses.

On the other hand, this same person was jealous of the fact that she had to go to work every morning and I didn't, jealous of the fact that I make more money sleeping than she was making with extra hours, and jealous of everything I know. Despite this, her jealousy, as you can see, was making her poor.

Jealousy also made her grow in hatred, which then led to emotional revenge, in the form of partying alone with her friends, and insulting me in what regards all of her options for meeting someone else, and this, after we had many discussions about it. As a result, I then proceeded on my way to another country and had to leave her behind. She lost the house she had with me and went back to sleeping in a room, lost the opportunity to get married, and lost the possibility of not needing a job anymore, simply by being married to me and traveling the world with me. She lost all of that, which she told me was her big dream since early childhood, because of her poverty mindset, filled with hatred and jealousy, which obviously, attracts more of the same, i.e., attracting other people like her, who are also poor, full of hate and jealousy.

Her friends persuaded her to party with them and find another boyfriend, by badmouthing me, and because her energy vibrates at the same frequency as theirs — scarcity and hate, she trusted such friends and lost everything she actually wanted.

So many times this girl has said: "I don't know what I did to deserve you in my life"; and maybe never will she know, but she certainly knows now what she did not to deserve me anymore.

In fact, one of the most common assumptions that people tend to make, is in believing that if the majority trusts them, if their friends support them, this makes them correct and even an expert of something by default, either it is a group of friends, a group of people attending a seminar, or those at home watching a TV show. But what is a fool approving another fool? Aren't they both fools? A blind man talking to another blind man, will never change the fact that they are both blind, despite agreeing on everything they say about themselves and reality.

The Realm of False Religions

In believing that the religious God, no matter which religion it is, is the God of the poor, the ignorant and the arrogant, because they make the majority, those who follow such beliefs are guided on the opposite direction of what they consider themselves to be, as their own heart shows to those who can see it. They are also damaging their own faith, and impoverishing their soul. And there is no better way to notice it as in their own words, for they are often composed of delusional faith, i.e., a strong belief in things they can't properly explain.

I have studied the bible and many other religious books during my entire life, and know for a fact that the Biblical God, the Hindu God, the Islamic God, as many other Gods, all despise poverty, sickness and ignorance. And I have written many books proving it too.

It is actually interesting that many christians still believe this, as it was an idea promoted by catholicism for tax purposes, and to enforce a social hierarchy on the people, just as it still happens today with many other ideologies sponsored by those in power, among which the most popular has certainly been the western view on feminism and communism.

Nobody will ever tell you that the God of any religion wants everyone to prosper and be wealthy, because this goes against two strong motivators in the world — fear and jealousy, i.e., the fear of the rich in losing what they have, and the jealousy of the poor in failing to get it.

To think that the rich are all evil is also actually a very stupid assumption, as much as believing that the poor are good people. But many poor people from around the world, especially, most South Americans I know, want me to believe that, while forgetting that terrorism and violent revolutions always come from the hands of the poor.

Obviously, we could say that rich people control the world and use money to fund terrorist organizations and instigate revolutions, but who is more stupid, the one who tells you to slap the face of someone else, or you for doing it because someone else asks you? And who is more violent, the one who gives you a gun to shoot, or you for using the gun and shooting?

All evil comes from the hands of the poor; not the rich. And even though both rich and poor can steal, one threatens your life when stealing you merely coins, while the other can't rob you without breaking the law, and may take much more, but at least allows you to live. And how much would you pay to be alive?

I have even heard other absurd things from religious individuals, such as: "A christian sister gave me the keys to her house and I did not have to pay for anything." Sure not, but that same sister, was rich enough to own more than one house, and not need to rent it too. A poor person doesn't have such an abundance to give freely.

The same imbecile that said this, then told me: "Once I was welcomed by a poor family in Mexico and they gave me a soup." And, regarding that, I can only answer the following: "Once I offered plenty of money to a beggar, and he invited me to sit by his side and talk to him on the floor."

He then continued, asking me if I know many rich people, trying to insinuate that the poor are more friendly. And to this, I answered: "I rather be alone than have friends always insulting me for being ambitious and enjoying the lifestyle that they can't have because they are poor; and I also rather be alone, than to be insulted all the time by someone jealous of my potential, either it is a friend, a spouse or a family member."

Rich people don't have friends, because the majority is imbecile, jealous and full of hatred, especially, the poor. How do you think I feel when I am having lunch with family members, and they insult me for being able to travel to the Phillipines and Thailand whenever I want, with words like "I work very hard every day and earn very little, and can't even afford to travel outside Europe"? Should I feel guilty for their misery? Should I hate myself for having what they don't? None of that! That's pure jealousy and hatred! And what should I say about family members who are constantly telling me stories about people who were rich and got arrested, implying that all the rich do something illegal to get their wealth? It is pleasant to spend any time with such people? Certainly not!

That is why I have no friends or family. And even though I can't just rebuild a family, I can make new friends, and I do, all the time, because I am a very social person, and very outgoing, and talkative. I make an average of five hundred friends a year. That's how fast I am. Then, I remove them all from my life, or they remove themselves after failing to change me into the crap person they wish me to become; and at the end, from those five hundred, I get about two that can still maintain a normal conversation without insulting me or trying to make me poor. And I can assure you, that they come from all religious and cultural backgrounds.

This resumes the explanation to why the rich are always alone. They are not selfish, but simply aware of what a disgusting bunch the masses are. Selfishness is how the poor perceive them. And certainly, I have been called selfish many times too, for not wanting to share what I know, or not accepting "advice" and "help" that intended to destroy my lifestyle. Naturally, whenever I refuse poisonous gifts, I am accused of either being selfish or arrogant, by those who are jealous and imbecile themselves.

The Realm of False Spirituality

Money does not make people evil, and if anyone thinks that I should not get more from life because that person thinks I will become evil, then this person is not my friend, but a Devil Worshipper, as only Satan wants me miserable. Satan is the god of the stupid, the imbecile, the uneducated, the arrogant, the mentally ill and the poor. And I do not say this out of naiveness. I have written nearly four hundred books, naturally, not because I am stupid, but because I have very high researching skills. I have studied quite a lot of religions, enough to see that the biblical God is the same of all other religions. The problem of religion, is a problem of human thinking, and not God.

The mental problem that people face with this theory comes mostly from poor countries like those in South America, because they have witnessed a lot of poverty. But there is a big difference between being a good person and being afraid. You do not pay taxes because you want to do good but because you are afraid of the consequences. And the same occurs with those who are afraid to oppose the God of their religion.

This whole world operates on fear, not goodness. Very few people would remain good in a world without laws. That is why we need the laws. The purpose of a law is to replace moral, because most human beings do not have any ethics or self-discipline. They do not have any way to restrain themselves when permitted to do evil in the world.

This said, I seriously doubt that a person that can't understand complex and abstract meanings about reality, is able to fully understand spirituality and religion, including his own. And that makes him unqualified to teach me or anyone else on anything of what regards faith. I obviously include here the speakers and the preachers of many congregations.

There are different types of poverty, not just one. But you would have to read many more books of mine to understand that part. Financial poverty is just one of them; You also have lack of education, lack of ethics, and many more forms of misery.

On the other hand, I do believe that anyone can be qualified in something, no matter how rich or poor, but is not because I was a teacher for many years that I can teach Quantum Physics to anyone. One thing doesn't imply the other.

Those who are more spiritual, are also blessed with more light in them, but quite often they don't trust themselves, and are easily manipulated by the arrogant, who pretend to know better, and that's how the truth ends up distorted, despite its foundations. When a spiritual person trusts what others tell him, rather than himself, he is ignoring the gifts that God gave him. And whenever such individuals are trying to teach me that poverty is a good thing and the rich are evil, then I am not interested in hearing anything from them or their religion any longer, because that type of faith is false.

Money does not make people evil. The ones who tell you that, are they, themselves evil, and projecting jealousy unto others. Because they don't have enough money, and can't learn how to make more. In every single person who has shown me hatred towards wealth, I witnessed jealousy and resentment. The misinterpretation comes from their own suffering, and suffering makes people jealous, stupid and evil. And of course, if they see someone else making more money than them, they then think that such person is helped by Satan. It's the logic of idiots. Because if that person is part of their congregation, they typically believe the exact opposite, i.e., that he is being blessed because he is more virtuous.

The fools are always chasing superficial logics created by their own superficial mentality.

The Dangers of Radicalism

I have heard many members of the Jehovah Witnesses telling me, or implying, that I am probably possessed by the Devil, because I write too many books. But what if not? What if I am a prophet? What if the bible is not complete? What if God speaks to me to correct the stupidity of all religions in this world and give a chance to those who have no other? What if I am writing books to correct the misinformation being spread and guide people back to God? What if my words are the only complete truth available right now that anyone can access without singing a bunch of nonsense on a congregation, or being misguided by the arrogance of groups of fools?

You see, the vast majority of the christians nowadays is so arrogant, and have such a polluted heart, that I have no doubt that God wants nothing with them. Because, you know, I love my parents, but I want nothing with them either. I do pity the evil ones, and the jealous and the crazy, but I want nothing with them either. And if God made Man in his image, I am sure God behaves the same. His love for humanity doesn't imply forgiving someone who's heart is closed by arrogance.

Any religion claiming that God likes people to be poor, sick and stupid, and not read anything else but one book, or not work hard enough but be contempt with little, while seeing in sickness a virtue, is not only a false religion, but a religion followed by idiots.

If the bible is a book containing truth, I must say then, that the Jehovah Witnesses are very far from being able to teach it. And when someone tries to teach me something that they don't understand, they do worse than not doing anything. Because, likewise, I am not an Engineer, and therefore, I am not trying to build bridges.

Simply putting it, a person that doesn't understand the bible, should not teach it. And I don't care what kind of excuses they have, if they are struggling with their life or going through financial problems, because, also, no excuse will serve any good, if I was driving a car and hit a bunch of pedestrians on the way for the same reasons.

So far, every single person that I have met, in more than thirty countries, does not understand anything about the bible, and shows an incredible level of arrogance as I have never seen before. In particular, the vast majority of the Jehovah Witnesses, are extremely arrogant beyond belief. And the more someone shows them that, the more they rejoice on it, thinking that if someone attacks them so much, their God must love them a lot. It is the same logic of the schizophrenic who thinks there is a conspiracy theory to stop him from killing innocents by bombing himself in public and fulfill God's will.

If Christ came to Earth right now, I am sure he would not want anything to do with more than 90% of the people in any christian congregation, or any other.

The Patterns of Misinterpretation

To believe that God only likes the poor and despises the rich is probably the best indicator of how little anyone understands the bible or any other religious book. And every single christian, buddhist, scientologist or islamic that I have met, showing this mindset, usually also shows a very high level of arrogance, accompanied by too much ignorance at the same time; because these two things are indeed a perfect match. And that is why I lose my patience all the time with such people: I do not study religious knowledge to become more stupid; I don't read books to become stupid; I don't work to become poor. These ideas can only come from the mind of someone who is mentally ill.

We also don't live to die, i.e., the purpose of a congregation is not to escape Armageddon but to live, and the two reasons are very different, although they sound the same, because they drive people towards different motivations.

Most people are completely insane because they think in this way, that somehow they are special because they dress well every Saturday to pretend they are good persons. But the vast majority is not, and any mainstream test from psychology could show it. But that's why they hate someone who knows more, as those who know more, expose them for who they really are; and most christians are too arrogant to confess their spiritual limitations. Whenever someone knows too much and can see too much, that person is, according to them, always somehow guided by evil, because they want to keep on believing that they are good. It's the same logic of the soccer fans: "If you don't support my team, you are not my friend."

I respect good intentions, but good intentions with a polluted heart, pollute the world in the name of good. Most of the christians are too far away from being at the level of helping anyone. And I am not necessarily the type of individual who is easily brainwashed, but that's what the way they teach is — brainwashing. There is not logic; only forced stupidity, which when rejected, is resented.

You know, christians, and other groups, could do a very good job, if they were doing the work of God. They are not anymore. The heart of the majority has been polluted and corrupted. And if they think spirituality and money are not related topics, they certainly have not seen how their lack of wealth has made them bitter and resentful, which then led them to propagate a message that distorts the truth that God certainly wants people to have.

I don't know how it really happened, but there is too much evil inside congregations feeding on the arrogance and the sense of entitlement of the majority. And yet, whoever tries to teach others but is not spiritually prepared, ends up insulting without knowing it. And for me, arrogance is always very insulting. Because arrogance hides resentment and resentment perverts the mind, and corrupts the heart. And even those who are not arrogant, do tend to fall into this trap, if put there by someone else who guides them in the wrong way.

I do understand that it is hard to find the right people, as even I have done many mistakes too in trying to find them. I have trusted many people in whom I should not trust. But if one is honest with himself, doesn't take long to identify his own mistakes.

If anyone, for example, tries to compete with me in intelligence and knowledge in the field of spirituality, he will most likely lose, not because I am smarter or even because I have much more knowledge, but because I have studied enough and have been guided for too long, and was also spiritually attacked by too many people who are possessed, to fall victim of deception.

God, through his miracles and opportunities, has helped me in seeing the truth, as much as the Devil did, through the type of people he has chosen to possess, and the type of things he told me, through these same individuals, to try to destroy me and stop me from doing what I am doing now. In this sense, I probably know the real God better than most people. That, doesn't mean I am better than others, but certainly makes me different in many ways. The fact that I am the one writing all these gospels in the form of books, while those who claim to be guided by God and enlightened can't, most surely makes me unique.

How God Blesses His Followers

I am always under attack, and It is very difficult for me to live as I do, on my own. But God blessed me with wealth, and this wealth allows me to move, escape, travel and be free to withdraw from evil in any form. And so, whoever tries to take this away from me, is following the way of the Devil. And many members of the Jehovah Witnesses, even though considering themselves the chosen ones, are more influenced by the Devil than they are by God. And I do respect their spiritual problems, but they have not come out of them to be able to teach anyone else. Nobody's life or past justifies imbecility.

My life has always been extremely hard and painful at many levels. I did not become who I am today, without having to go through more suffering than most people on this planet can handle. This is how I got to know Satan. I have been attacked by Satan through possessed people during my entire life, and so much, that at one point I started knowing the signs, and predicting them too, before the attacks begun. Today, I can literally walk on any street of the world, and know who is evil, who is stupid, who is possessed, and who is good and blessed, just by feeling people's energy, and confirming it with their facial structure and eyes. This is why I know today as well, that I rather hear foolishness from a highly spiritual person, than hear very good theories from a very arrogant and wicked individual. I do not trust humans with polluted souls and dark hearts full of rage.

When I choose to trust one person, that person is receiving a gift. When this person damages my trust, it is like stepping on that gift. As I was betrayed all my life, I have learned a lot about the human nature. And so, I do not trust anyone easily. And I spend a lot of my time alone because I trust almost nobody in fact. I can see people for who they are, and my values are very high. If God had to finish humanity right now, I would probably be very accurate in helping Him choose which ones to go and which ones to stay. That is why I am blessed with so much knowledge, and that is why I am always under spiritual attack too.

Now, everyone does mistakes, but there are different types of mistakes, and you surely don't want to be deceived by someone with a dark soul, because those mistakes are often motivated by very perverse motives which are also extremely difficult to identify and defend against. A possessed individual, for example, will attack you precisely on your greatest weaknesses, and make you question the validity of your own life purpose, without you even noticing that such attack has just happened. The best among them, attack you with politeness, claiming that they are doing it because they want the best for you. These are the ones saying things like: "Don't just settle down before having sex with more people"; "Don't work so hard because you need to enjoy your life as well"; "Give yourself a chance, even when someone is very evil and disrespectful"; "Get drunk and smoke drugs while you are young"; and my favorite: "Money is not the most important thing".

I like this last quote in particular because it is the most common and the most vicious. It is also particularly interesting, for the fact that, those who say that money is not the most important thing in life, are also not the most trustworthy friends or the most loving ones. Many of them struggle financially too, or live from charity. The last person who told me, for example, this lives with her parents. Obviously, for her, money is not the most important thing; the charity of her parents is. And that brings me to another obvious fact about those who say that money is not important: They are selfish. Because, only a person who is not selfish, sees the meaning of hard work and money, and knows that money can't be made without work, a type of work that benefits others.

It is actually very offensive the way poor people ask me how I make money, because they are usually trying to find specific strategies and tricks, and never believe me whenever I talk about hard work. Many people asking me about how to sell books, for example, never read any of mine. That is why they show no respect for what I do. They are merely trying to learn how to sell garbage to the world, and insulting me while doing it.

It may take a while, but you do need to see if a person, preacher, author, or simply a guru, is really interested in your spiritual learning or something else, beyond his own selfish motives. And because money is probably the best indicator of how spiritual someone is, allow me to teach you the following: If money is important for you, you will want to make more, and you can earn more; if you do, you can do more, including create your own business and expand your company beyond yourself, employing more people, then raising their salary, and taking more human beings out of what is, most likely, permanent unemployment. And what is bad about wanting to do so much good and expand this good in the world?

If you think, or even suspect, that God doesn't want you to make more money, you are worshiping the wrong God, and not helping anyone else, not even yourself. Charity is a very good thing when you receive it, but it is much better when you are the one giving it to others. And if you are being enlightened by the right God, you will easily see the meaning of my words.

About the Publisher

This book was published by the 22 Lions Bookstore.
For more books like this visit www.22Lions.com.
Join us on social media at:
Fb.com/22Lions;
Twitter.com/22lionsbookshop;
Instagram.com/22lionsbookshop;
Pinterest.com/22LionsBookshop.

www.ingramcontent.com/pod-product-compliance
Lightning Source LLC
Chambersburg PA
CBHW050451010526
44118CB00013B/1778